IN BED WITH ANIMALS

By the same author:

Between Worlds (2023)

IN BED WITH ANIMALS

BRONWYN LOVELL

RECENT
WORK
PRESS

In Bed With Animals
Recent Work Press
Canberra, Australia

Copyright © Bronwyn Lovell, 2022

ISBN: 9780645356342 (paperback)

A catalogue record for this book is available from the National Library of Australia

Cover image: Image from page 58 of 'What happened then stories' (1918) by Ruth O Dyer and Florence Liley Young.
Cover design: Recent Work Press
Set by Recent Work Press

recentworkpress.com

EF

For Carmela, who changed everything

Contents

PART IV

Cautionary Note

Dear reader, please be advised that this collection of non-fictional truth-telling poems raises serious concerns about sexual discrimination, harassment, and violence, as well as their subsequent mental health impacts. Please take care while reading—and living—this disturbing social reality.

PART I

Insomnia

The hoarding started young.
I had a lot of dolls I wanted
to be lost among. When
preparing for bed, I piled them
high on my pillow and buried

myself below, so when the man
came in the night to take me,
he might lift the smiling clown
with plaited pigtails and snatch
her soft body instead of mine.

I never could sleep for the metal
clock ticking with its panda heads
duly nodding along, coerced
by some hidden mechanism.
Each click was a steel-capped

boot scraping closer to my door.
Mama panda knew she couldn't
clutch her cub forever. My mum
read me the 'It's OK to Say
No' series—stories that teach

children how to survive our wild:
when the man touches you, pulls
you towards the car, wants you
to keep secrets, it's OK to say, 'No!'
Happy endings showed savvy

kids confiding in trusted adults
who made everything OK. But
Mum's voice gave the pretence
away. My room was at the front
of the house, nearest the street.

I would be the lamb when
the man came and the panda
clock my grandparents had gifted
was merely counting down
to the time he would force me,

even if I were brave enough
to voice my no. He was already
on his way. He had come for my
mum, my aunt, my nan before
me. No, it's not OK. Not at all.

A girl's compendium of hairy stories [abridged]

on the way to school when the man
on the bus presses his body firm
against my nine-year-old form

and I shuffle across to give him
more room but he keeps taking
mine till I can no longer move

any closer to the window or fold further
in on myself I shake in every sinew
pinned silent like an accordion with no air

***

at the swimming carnival it's compulsory
to compete but I am starting to develop
at twelve and would rather keep my fledgling

breasts, wobbly thighs and belly flops to myself
why aren't you swimming Mrs Campbell asks
we've got our periods my friends and I say

show me she demands suspiciously and
escorts the lot of us into the toilet block
to pull down our pants

***

at seventeen on a school trip
a chuckling man's hand thrusts
up my skirt on the street

I scream
my French teacher yells at me
for causing a scene

***

in my last year of high school
my sailing instructor hands me
vodka that tastes like lemon squash

guides me behind the dunes
and tries to kiss me
he was sixty

***

I leave the Navy abruptly
after the ship's Chief Engineer
quizzes me on all matters of my virginity

employing grotesque gestures and imagery
to thoroughly degrade and humiliate me
in front of six senior officers

for his Saturday night entertainment
and when the Captain seeks an explanation
for my sudden resignation

he concludes I am mistaken
because the accused is his close friend
of more than two decades

***

at the interview the gallery owner
seeks assurance against my biology
how do I know you won't just go

and get yourself pregnant?
I am nineteen and don't understand
how being pretty is a liability

for long-term employability
I admit to having a boyfriend
and don't get the job

***

in my twenties a taxi driver in Turkey
helps himself to my vagina and purse
but it could have been so much worse

***

sometimes when I say sorry
someone will say stop apologising
and I will say sorry

the word was beaten into me
the daughters of angry men
say sorry like an incantation

***

in my thirties the uni counsellor suggests
we compose the email to my supervisor
together how will you start she asks

dear ▓▓▓ [same name as my brother] I sob
I'm sorry for the misunderstanding
stop she interrupts do not say sorry

do not claim responsibility
for his coming onto you
this is a linguistic revelation

in female expression but still
should I say how sorry I am again
about his breastless dead wife

***

at my nephew's second birthday party
when my brother's friend enquires
after me romantically my brother warns

him off says she's a real feminist now
feminist or feminazi my teenage cousin
asks and how they laugh

now I'm not gunning
for genocide on that gender
of dicks but if

I'd been there I would have shot them all
down then helped my sister-in-law
scrub their dirty plates

***

as a lecturer in my forties
unpacking popular culture
with young adults

student survey remarks suggest
a little less feminism in class
would be nice

***

In the end it's not the wolf
that kills you though it's true he would
dress in your grandmother's corpse

for a fuck I've let him come
in more than once but it's the pigs
who finally defeat you

common uncunning little shits
and their torrent of sticks and bricks
blowing you down again and again

Bitching

When you were a baby, I left you
home alone all day and you cried
and cried and I'm so sorry I didn't
know then what dog love was.

After our neighbour complained,
my partner ordered a shock collar
online and tried to convince me it
wasn't cruel, while you, poor pup,

didn't understand why you were
being zapped. He wouldn't pick up
poo or come on walks and when
you piddled on the rug he told me

I had to give you up. I saw he
wasn't dad material. You saved
offspring from the shock of life
with a father who pays more

attention to the television than
the wriggling of the living—a man
who values stereo system
wiring above mewling, teething

creatures. You rescued me from
the rut of that relationship. I say
that gravely. I know you were fond
of him, even though he yelled

at you, made you quiver with fear,
cower in the corner of the kitchen.
My dad says dogs are dumb. If
a man kicks one, it will come back

to be kicked again. I have been
that kind. The behaviourist tells
me my dog has a mental illness.
Your attachment to me is crazy.

Five different anxiety pills effective
on four out of five dogs and none
of them work for you. Because
you are shaking in the backseat

I am trying to be quick at the
supermarket, which means I will
forget things and line up too soon
because I know you are waiting

for me in dog minutes, beating out
your canine heart. Twenty-five
minutes to me is two-and-a-half
hours to you. A lifetime to you is

a decade and a half maybe to me.
I fear your death will kill me.
Anxiety is just one of the ailments
we share. Desexing can spur

incontinence. I leak too. You know
because of your nose. It's one of
our secrets. I too am de-partnered
and de-sexed but not desperate.

Although there is desperation.
High-maintenance, clingy, needy
—all words lovers have used
to criticize me. I am dogged by

my doppelganger. I coax your
frantic form to calm with treats.
I speak commands firmly past
my own panic, trying not to inflect

at the end like so many
women, such that statements
become questions as though
even we don't quite believe

our words are worth heeding?
We are used to being ignored;
we are wounded and scorned.
Some dog days feel like years.

Efforts repeat and yield no! no!
no! reward. My beast and I are
training to settle down, to not
react, to be good girls and distrust

our instincts. To not bark. To not
bite. To let the indignities bead
and shake them off like bullets
flung from a wet dog's back.

We will not howl; we've learnt
to yearn without a whimper.
We are both on anti-depressants
because we get diarrhoea when

we're nervous and we don't like
strangers around the house.
Doctors ask about the bruises.
Am I in an abusive relationship?

No, although I am loved violently.
You collide with my body. Your
pounding paws imprint yellow
purple and green. You get under

my skin. I have so many tender
spots for you. I am struck
by the force of your affection.
You bring into stark reflection

the lack of passion in past loves
and that too packs a sting.
I am more to you than I've ever
been to anyone or will be again.

You don't mind if from time
to time I fail to rise and neglect
to raise the blinds. I ken
the comfort of closing my eyes

in a den heavy with darkness
and warm bodies that stink of
compost and dung and the filth
of living. If I masturbate beside

the dog there will be no judgement,
just snuggles afterwards. Last night
I dreamt you leapt the fence and
I watered the bed with a flood

of dread. I was too sluggish to change
the sheets, but you were sweet
enough to sleep mutely in the wet
spot. I don't bother dolling or dating.

I am not me in human company.
Dog people are the best people.
They don't mind hairs on clothes
or mud on the furniture and they

aren't precious about the carpet.
They mop up the mess of life's
accidents without fuss. They
understand that all bodies

make mistakes, sounds and smells.
They realise we're mere mammals.
You bring in leaf litter and dust
from my neglected garden. I too

am a messy animal. Threads
of my hair spiral with yours
in the vacuum as we shed dead
cells, minutely remake ourselves.

I throw the ball; you bring it
back. There's comfort in that
sense things thrust from us can
be retrieved. Some balls we find

another day, others not at all.
My backyard is a graveyard
of buried toys and chalky dung
baked hard in the kiln of the sun.

Instinctively, my dog and I speak
the same language. We exchange
grumbles and sighs. We dislike
passers-by, revved up cars, cock

our heads down the cul-de-sac
and raise hackles at the dead-
end neighbours. We guard our own
territory, this fort of familiar ground.

Outside, the real mums yell at me
from their happy families, perched
on plaid picnic blankets. *Put your
dog on a lead; we've got children!*

You are my only child. Besides,
it's an off-leash park and their kids
are on the play equipment and you
are not interested in them, just

the fairy bread they've left behind.
I don't say anything in our defence
and you don't eat the candied bread
because I tell you not to and you're

better trained than most. When I
was a child, my mum buckled
me into a leather leash to go
to the shops because I'd always

take off. You would never leave
me like that. I am not your real mother.
I am not a good one either. I barely
manage myself. When you dig

down with your deep eyes, I sense
you comprehend this. Recently you
caught up and overtook me in dog years.
You have begun to mother me, lick

my crusty eyes open gently
of a morning. I like your old lady
noises, am soothed by the rhythmic
lull of soft flatulence and light snoring.

We domestic animals are still wildly
frightened. If a man mauls me,
they will look for the predator's DNA
carved in crescents under my claws.

If I do it myself, finally, along the vein,
you, my dear, will lap up the syrup—
salty, warm and iron-deficient. Promise
to eat me when I die. I'd much

rather sustain you than decompose
till somebody notices. Your maw
is friendlier than funeral fire. Help me
skip the lonely box, depressing speech.

We have a pact. We are pack. I feed
you and you look out for me, watch
the window while I lie naked, growl
our hollow warning into the night.

New South Welsh

Here I am alive
where colonists buried

the copious
unjustly dead

down the yard
past the old milk truck

picking cherry tomatoes
with my little brother.

Here I am where we began
as usual all out of time

by the incinerator,
Nanna's head

bent in a swan tyre
slashed full of geraniums,

the creek a siren call
shelled in concrete graffiti.

Here we are feeding white
ducks with labrador smiles.

Here we are waving
to police helicopters

before knowing
what it's really like to fly,

before feeling the cold sting
of altitude, hard buffet of blades.

Here I am under Nan's oak tree,
imagining friends to be less lonely.

Here I am in a steel
shipping container marked

with an identifying number.
Here I am at the cape

of another country
in the middle of a dream

where I can't keep hold
of anything and seagulls scream

like abandoned children.
I do not know from where

my ancestors came,
if not this Celtic crag

then surely sprung from some
precarious life perched

on the precipice where all
the windblown grasses know

is to weather whatever hits
and do this one thing well.

Working girl

I trade time for dollars at the minimum
wage exchange. I wipe tables instead

of writing poems. I am well versed
in the cycle of reheating and eating

frozen meals in the windowless staff
room. I know my worth in hourly

increments. I have purchased property
with my body. I have a small patch

of grass the bank lets me mow. I live
within my fence, make my garden

pretty, iron my uniform to hang an
empty effigy to my hollow shape.

I am paying the bank off for a metal
box in which I cart myself across

suburbs pumping noxious gas exhaust
on my way to the shopping centre

where I serve the fried flesh of dead
animals to pigs who don't think they

are animals. I scrape the waste from
their plates into the trash to be shipped

out to stink up some other place
where garbage piles like body bags.

ii.

I want to do the real work—I want
to write the world anew but that's

not what companies pay me to do.
I am the overqualified unskilled.

I am the doctoral student you drive
-thru, that see-through counter chick.

Sometimes I wonder what lipstick,
wig, tit tassels and a spray tan might

do. How much could I make? What
would it strip from me and could I

break even, pay my way out? What's
a small heart-sink for cash in hand?

iii.

I see how it happens—an overdue
power bill, medication for the cat,

funding cuts, no penalty rates, my
savings account stripped bare.

There isn't a woman in my lineage
who hasn't earned her keep.

Stripper me does not differ greatly
from strapped me. She's just a girl

trying to make some money. She's
simply more practical: writes off

fish-net stockings and pole-dancing
classes on her tax. It wouldn't take

much—full body wax, theatre-thick
foundation, waterproof mascara

and a spine. The girls without
scholarships do it; call them

entrepreneurial. Call me by my name
badge, 'Love', or something else entirely.

Fucking lucky

because in my worst
experience of assault
it was a dirty hand
that stabbed
its way up my vagina,
not a penis or knife
and because it was one
man, not the gang
of friends he rang and
because I was only
gone for an hour
not days or years
and instead of joining
the realms of missing
women drugged
bashed, trafficked
or otherwise
deprived of their lives
I was dropped
off physically intact,
dizzy and livid

Our friend ███
[same name as my uncle]

You know him or someone like him.
He's the kind of man you'd call decent.
Politically left, feminist, generous.
He has a wealth of female friends, one

of whom introduced us. Last Christmas,
I told her I didn't like how he'd touched
me when she went to get the car but
she seemed to dismiss my concerns

because I was drunk and he had been
her friend for far longer. The man was
esteemed by such smart, sharp women,
that I too shelved my misgivings till his

hand slid up my back one night in sudden
reminder. I confided once more in my
friend and only then did she divulge
that some months earlier he had tried

to coax her into his bed and she no longer
meets with him except in the company
of friends and would I please not tell
any of them. So, it must happen again.

Killer

Ever since I encountered the bikie
who complimented my eyes and
tried to fondle me at a rest stop
on the Western Highway, I have
wanted a Doberman called Killer.

When I called for my dog that day,
voice shaking as I quickstepped
back to the car, her name did not
seem threatening enough; it was
labrador lovely, whippet weak.

Carmela was too sweet in her pink
diamante collar devoid of studs.
Forty kilometres down the road,
sure I was not being followed,
I pulled over and rang my dad.

He said I should expect to be hit
on by men because I was young
and pretty. I've aged now and
put on some weight, so maybe
I'm safe. I still want a Doberman.

I would spell her name K-H-I-L-A,
which means 'blooming' in Hindi.
I always thought having a dog
would protect me, but it didn't
shield Toyah Cordingley. Her dad

found her gentle shepherd tied
to a tree not far from her naked
body. Toyah was too pretty to walk
carefree along a quiet beach with
a dog that was not a killer—her

youth blooming, legs moving, heart
beating fast as her bare feet quick-
stepped across the sand, smiling
in that I-am-no-threat way, before
being hit on in the afternoon sun.

[same name as my kindergarten sweetheart]

I cringe when I see his photo in festival programs, his
books praised in progressive publications. No doubt
his writing deserves the attention. As a person of colour,
he is intimate with injustice and his voice is important.

However, he did not listen to mine the night he insisted
on coming inside after winning the poetry slam. I took
care to emphasise that all I could offer at that hour was
a quick chat and a cup of tea. He seemed to accept that

but then he began caressing my thigh. I moved away
repeatedly till he could see he wasn't going to get
what he had invited himself in for, and eventually
he left. I got into my pyjamas and went to bed.

But then I found myself letting him back in.
He said he'd been locked out of his accommodation
and had nowhere to go, except I still don't know why
he didn't call one of his mates and leave me alone.

I wondered if he was like Michael Flatley and had some
sordid tradition of fucking women after the adrenaline
of the stage. I set him up on the couch and he was put
out by that. My bed was a queen and he didn't see

why he shouldn't be welcome in it. By morning, he
had slipped into my room and between the sheets.
By then, his sex-drive had been dulled by sleep. Still,
he would not relinquish his presumed right to my bed

despite my obvious distress and repeated requests.
I guess spending the night of the slam in bed with
a fan read as poetry for his winning reputation.
It was awful for mine. I had a boyfriend at the time.

I hate hearing him talk on the radio or TV, since
I know him to be so lamentably incapable of listening
to women. Meanwhile, our unsavoury stories replay
with no marketing, no microphone, and no applause.

How to hug a friend:
A guide for men

Keep your hands high.
Give a light pat
on the upper back.

'Pat' should not
be confused with 'caress';
know the difference.

The waist is a no-go.
If you touch skin
at the meeting

of your friend's
top and bottom
clothing, your hands

are too low
and you are not
a friend at all.

You can lean in
but do not linger.
Save the sloppy

kiss for your missus.
Keep your pelvis
to yourself.

Prayer for the girl
who is not a feminist

May you never have cause to become one.
May low-cut blouses invite only sun.

May no-one mistake your figure for your worth,
no fingers force their way up your skirt.

May you never have to guard your glass—
wake up groggy, grow up fast.

May your neighbourhoods all be well lit.
May you never go through with it

just to be polite. May your high heels click
quickly through the car park at night.

May your make-up not thicken to cover
a nasty bruise from a boozy lover.

May your pay cheque never be so low
that you cannot leave when you need to go.

May you fail to find your mother's pain
folded quietly in the linen press

and guess which man you love is to blame.
May you be skipped by statistics.

May your friends escape the cars unscathed
and all your daughters come home safe.

PART II

The emotional astronomer

cares for telescopes like mechanical pets
camps out with cameras and an aching neck
tints torchlight, dims his van brothel-red
waits for the Earth to move, the Moon to set
props a director's chair for the fade to black
can't factor his children's resentment
accepts the conditions, won't ask the sky why—

will not love a nebula less the tenth time
gets teary at a clear viewing of Alpha Centauri
feels things to which his wife won't relate
needs no chart to plot the now fragile arc
of a retired accountant's amateur star—
knows meteors will rain down consolation:
Jupiter a river pebble, Saturn a silky stone

Ham the Astrochimp

Like 007 or 99, you were No. 65;
they wouldn't name you
unless you survived,
couldn't risk the public
outcry if you died,
didn't want you to seem
any more like a child
than your small hominid form
already inherently suggested,
didn't want people getting
emotionally invested.
Still, among the handlers
you were known
jokingly as Chop Chop Chang,
although you were African.
Two-year-old toddler
chimpanzee, they trained
you with flashbulbs
and buzzing sounds, shocked
the soles of your sensitive feet,
rewarded you with banana pellets.
You rode on a Redstone rocket,
wore a spacesuit that saved you
when the capsule lost pressure.
You weren't just a passenger,
you pushed levers, had tasks,
performed as they asked.
After splashdown, recovered
by the USS Donner, you shook

the hand of the ship's commander,
posed dutifully for the camera
despite a swollen bruised nose.
Once the program was done
with you, they sent you to a zoo
where you died too soon
and they planned to stuff
your skin, put you on display
at the Smithsonian like the dogs,
but public sentiment suggested
that was wrong, so to avoid
negative press, they solemnly
buried your fur and flesh
at the International Space Hall
of Fame, having already quietly
claimed your skeleton
for another museum collection.

Félicette

She was the first kitty in space—she flew
on a chic rocket called Véronique.
They chose her from fourteen
because she was so sweet.
She was the first feline
to experience weightlessness
(she didn't like it)
and the only one launched to make it back
alive. She was a tuxedo cat: black
and white like old photographs and silent
movies. She was classic—a classy
street cat with a Parisian pout.
She signed portraits with an elegant paw-print
in ink beside a handwritten note
(she must have dictated it).
Three months after her flight,
they killed her to cut up
her little brain with a knife
and study it in slices.

Doppler shift

Comes a time when your childhood bedroom is for guests
instead of a memorial to the little person you used to be (who remains
bigger in many ways than the grownup you've grown up to be),

when letters and treasures are packed away and your childish dreams
sleep quiet as boxes in your parents' garage. Here is the room
you could run to, shutting the door on any confrontation. Now,

the sore realization that even these few square metres were never yours.
So you cling to that disintegrating stuffed toy through the cold night
even though you're too old, in this house you can navigate in darkness

because its blueprints are under your skin like veins
cycling back to your deep thrombus heart.
You check if your father is still breathing when he falls

asleep in his armchair during a football match, this man who used to shout
and spit at the television till his face was red, and often at you, but thank Christ
these days leather belts merely hitch trousers to his increasingly shrinking form.

One day, you will find yourself back here, sorting
through your father's things with your elderly mother,
having to bury the argument

with his body, a stranger you knew well enough
to be afraid of but still loved furiously—
claws out like a kitten loves a fox.

Laika

Imagine the cruelty of that betrayal,
and the little window the scientists built
so she could see something magical
before her mission's fatal end.
A street dog, she lapped up the attention,
so grateful to be taken in, never guessing
how they planned to ship her out.
All that time, she tried to get it right.
Good girl. That's the way
to die. Quietly. Let them take
the bark out of you. Let them fool you,
blunt your bite, disarm your defences
for the honour to live on in the propaganda
of postage stamps, mass militaria and cheap
ornaments. There were other pups,
ones who survived the trip, who, riddled
with radiation, fell back to Earth, to endure
the excruciation of crumbling jaws and suck
the soft sausage meat of their hand-fed
retirement. Poor mutts with their mugs
plastered on plates and collectible coffee cups,
big toothy-grin photographs taken before
the terror of take-off,
before gentle natures and smiling
for cameras cost them their teeth.

Svetlana

Daughter of a Second World
War fighter pilot, she began parachuting
in secret at the age of sixteen
and was setting stratosphere jump records
before jetting off
to flight school.
As a member of the Soviet
aerobatics team, Svetlana flew
with an all-female crew to win
the world championship in 1970.
Taking her career
as a flight engineer to even greater
heights, she qualified as a cosmonaut.
Entering Salyut 7 for the first time, she found
that Anatoly and Valetin had prepared a special
welcome: they presented her with an apron,
pointed to the station kitchen
and said, snickering,
'Sveta, get to work.'
She was the first woman to spacewalk.

Western tropes

He will win her over like a bucking horse;
she will be broken, reined in and taught
to tolerate being ridden by him. She will
endure the whip and spurs, come to respect
the barbed fence, grow docile and almost
content to be his conquest, or so suggests
every epic frontier romance. Still, some cow-
boys think 'no' is not the end but merely
the beginning of a spirited negotiation
with a stubborn, fractious female.

When a woman says 'no', it is not an invitation
to change her mind. Let her go; she is so tired.
She dreams of a life without men on her back.

PART III

The Woodcutter's daughter

I have stopped fighting
the witch. Tired, I let her
in. I tried for years to deny
her entry, disgusted by

the cauliflower warts
sprouting between her toes.
To my horror, still they grow.
This crone festers in my

home. Filth gathers under
fingernails. Long, wiry
hairs spiral from moles.
Her mane is a flytrap,

her mouth a den of
yellowed teeth. Her lips
crack and her tongue
is thorned. Her scabby

skin prickles. Her arms
are cat-scratched, her face
hangs haggard with jowls.
At night she howls, drives

me to drink. Waterlogged
eyes sink in sooty cauldrons.
Dogs bark. Foxes prowl.
Shelves fill with spells.

Water burns. Sun stings.
Bones pile in the dustbin
all while she is cackling,
singing. She is preheating

the oven. She has scared
away the children. I eat
all the candy myself—
crumbless and brotherless.

Hoarder

I thought I'd never climb out but I took the pills prescribed learned to recognise DIS-ORDER inside did what the doctor ordered and was shocked when stockpiled plastic bottles filled a garbage bag I'd been saving slops of conditioner it's expensive can't afford to throw money away can't afford to live like this but DIS-ORDER keeps on creeping back purrs cold comforts smiles a shoebox full of faded photographs holds me close as trinkets carried all the way from childhood clings like musty dusty treasures stocks up on supermarket sale items prowls streets rescues vintage furniture chipped crockery discarded dresses abandoned ornaments from the side of the road and will mend them all one day DIS-ORDER hates visitors blocks them with latched gate barking dogs deadlocked door no one must see DIS-ORDER but me outside I present professionally push through workdays then spend weekends searching stacks for lost earrings boyfriends kids

Running into your ex

When it happens, be mindful how you label it.
Avoid words like 'fate' and 'destiny'. Say to yourself
'What a coincidence!' and think on it no more.

Do not calculate the odds of that city, that person,
that street; such mathematics leads only to madness.
Do not look to the heavens and imagine there

a great conductor; if there were such a musician
your mismatched tones would never have been
struck together again and again so carelessly.

Upon encountering that person in that city on that street
speak only briefly. Curb details. Do not dissect diction;
minced morphemes won't yield any answers.

Like a faulty set of kitchen scales you assign weight
too willingly; everything is heavier for you.
The only way to take this is lightly. Keep

eating and sleeping. Do not let your apartment
fall into disarray, nor re-enact the years
in fitful confusion. You can cry, even

glance back if you must, but do not abandon
your direction: walk on, surefooted. Turn
a corner, brave the empty signless street.

I have given up

on my boyfriend
which is sensible, since we broke up
some time ago
and only fair
since he did the same to me

I am no longer waiting for his taxi
to pull up outside my door
and I don't expect to trip on a bouquet
of forgive-my-fuck-up roses
when I step from my apartment

I am regaining a sense of self
hatred and the kilos
I lost to make him sorry

I am not waiting
I've just fallen
a little behind

If I still browse baby names
it's because I have an interest
in etymology and linguistics

I have given up on my boyfriend
but not as yet on me

See, I am taking vitamins
and brushing my teeth
mostly

I am not unhappy,
merely lacking
a particular kind of joy

Shop girl

if you are waiting for the right girl
the really truly special one who blows
your mind and cock and the girl shop
doesn't have her in yet you can take
a loan girl until the right one comes
and then you can return the other one
since they mostly dust off fine
you might just have to wait a long time
to buy the girl you're looking for
and even then she may not be available
straight away but thankfully
there are women like me
there are women who will let you
take them home with nothing sparkly
you can drive them round and round
for free while looking for a better one
there are women who will wait
in the passenger seat

Hornet in my kitchen

I didn't like the look of you,
back wrapped in caution tape
all orange and black, buzzing
frustration at my window

in many gentle collisions
until you gave up, retreated
to the bottom corner of the sill
to tuck your abdomen under

yourself, silent and still.
I don't know how a hornet
experiences emotion, but something
in the curve of you looked sad.

I would have pointed to the space
where my window opens
onto the world, and said, 'Look,
see here—this is your freedom'.

I wanted to rouse you
from that corner, but I
was too scared to touch you,
terrified of your sting.

What if you made your own cage

and you lived between
the mesh of the front and back
security screens, passing
days without saying a word
except perhaps the occasional
quiet expletive when you kick
your toe or consider the utter
meaninglessness of your
existence: *fuck*

what if you were allergic
to the dust but you didn't
vacuum so you coughed
and your parents and friends
had thankfully left you
to your miserable
moods behind the metal lattice
where you are locked in and free

to stay in your dressing gown
with unbrushed hair and teeth
and crawl into bed and doze
with the dog who won't judge
even though she'd rather
be at the park and might nudge
you gently to communicate this
but she won't push it

for which you are grateful
because you don't like
to be pushed and you don't
know how to kickstart your life
and besides there is something
nice about just closing your eyes
and the dog will not think less
of you and no one else will guess
at the mess behind the door
that is yours and yours alone

Sanctum

I call sweetly
but it's the cupboard
my cat likes best

snuggled at the back
of the bottom shelf
like a feather duster.

She can be enticed
but not forced
from this spot.

Secure within
straight surfaces
she feels are solid,

she can sleep
without being
disturbed.

I have spent years
curled up
beyond touch,

shrinking
comfortably
into shadows,

ears deaf
to my own
calling.

The future we want is already gone

I should have watered the garden
but I didn't. Things that were alive
are dead now because of me. And
this is not the first time. I have
enjoyed slaughtered animals in sauce—
sometimes by mistake, sometimes
knowingly. I have let men enter me,
mostly by mistake. I feed the animals
I keep in my house the heads and
hearts of other animals ground down
and baked into little cookies called
kibble. They eat it all and beg for
more. I cover my animal parts in cloth
made by people in other countries
in conditions called unlucky. I hang
a cruelty-free Christmas pig on my
plastic pine knowing a real tree died
for this cardboard display. We are
dysfunctional expressions of DNA.
Climate scientists say we're as good
as dead now anyway, but greedy as
cancer, we still gorge and grow—
exhausting everything, consuming
even ourselves.

Cycling

Like so many things
once unbroken and shiny,
my bike rusts on the front
verandah, tyres deflated.

There is always a reason
to sidestep the frame
chained to my porch:
I am tired, I don't have

the right pump or bolt.
My bike takes me
nowhere. I don't use it
because it doesn't work

and it doesn't work
because I don't use it
and it needs work,
like so many things

going nowhere: me,
my bike, rusting slowly.
I never could
get the gears right.

Fresh air, exercise,
these things help
the deflated, I know.
But I don't get on with it,

I don't get on my bike.
I sit inside, watch the box,
eat rubbish, don't
floss and fail to recycle.

Weekdays I hurry past
my bike, like so many
half-broken things
I sidestep each morning:

plants I could water,
litter I could lift to a bin,
beggars withering through
winter. In a solitary crowd

of commuters I write poetry
on the subway—words that
are unworthy of the forest
my notebook used to be.

Inside me, a bicycle's
tinny bell rings out.
I am alarmed
but not moved to action.

My resolutions rust
vermillion on the verandah;
spokes gather dust and
clutch at dead leaves.

PART IV

Phoning home

in memory of Alan Kurdi

i.

I am not so brave as Elliot, could never lay out
a candy path for hungry, lost forms to follow
through the dark to my bedroom door.

ii.

I'm in awe of this pale, awkward boy peddling
hard in little red hoodie, riding his bicycle across
the blue moon through crisp pine-needle night,
with the brown heart-shaped head of his small
alien friend blanket-cloaked in the basket up front,
pursued by sirens and uniforms, buoyed by love.

iii.

Often, you are alien to me. When our fingers touch
there's spark. You lift me over landscapes but I'm
afraid you'll let me fall. I have allowed the wrong
ones to carry me before. Let's just lie here on our
backs now, pedal each other's feet above the floor.

iv.

Together we must escape the Earthmen who land
stern as politicians in the driveway to set up
quarantine in space suits—an adult intervention
so sterile and inhuman, it turns us both white.

v.
You're killing him! Elliot shouts as E.T.'s heart
slows and stops in his small chalky chest.
The flowers droop and the body bag is zipped
and it's cold as frost but the corpse glows red.

vi.
If you are sick and I can't cure you, then we are both
sick. If you need family near you, I want them close
too. If sadness drifts in to settle ashen across your
face, then I must brave the boats, seek the mothership.

vii.
There will be times you will feel extraordinarily
lonely on this blue planet if you stay, my alien friend.
You'll see the broken father of a washed-up child
and understand that nature failed with human hearts.

Near Nannup, on our way to get hot cross buns

after W.H. Auden's *Musée des Beaux Arts*

About suffering they were never wrong,
The old Masters: how well they understood
Its human position: how it takes place
While someone else is texting or changing the radio station or just
    driving dully along;
How, when the queued cars are respectfully, patiently waiting
For the policewoman to wave them through, there always must be
Children who are excited by the flashing lights, fighting
In the backseat for a better view:
Auden knew, too,
That even the holiday road toll must run its course
Anyhow on a highway, some accident black spot
Where the cows go on munching dry grass and the dodged grey roo
Hops innocently past the fateful tree.

On this Easter long weekend, for instance: how everything turns away
Quite leisurely from the disaster; the farmer may
Have heard the crash, the rubber screech,
But for him it was not an important fence; the sun shone
As it had to on the pale feet disappearing under the white sheet, and the
    expensive delicate Porsche that must have seen
Something amazing, a yellow helicopter land in a field, a wreck
    wrenched open by the jaws of life,
Had somewhere to get to and sped calmly on.

Elsie

Even when she had forgotten everything, her body
remembered how to hold a hand.

It was horrible, the way she went.
She could have died better.

This is why humans need the idea of Heaven—
a coda, an epilogue, a where-are-they-now stipulation.
It's why we linger in the cinema after the credits of a disturbing
film; we hate things to end badly.

I remember the day my mother confirmed my worst fears:
Santa Claus wasn't real. Fairies fell from the sky—
their fragile bodies dropped as dead birds. Magic dissolved
like a painted backdrop: revealing a dull brick wall.

The death of God was less dramatic. My faith faltered—flashed
like a flickering streetlamp until the globe had nothing left.
I wanted to keep believing but it was no use. I'd outgrown
the fairy story, could no longer dangle
disbelief.

Still, I've known miracles. Have you thought
about our place in space recently?

I don't need God for myself. It's my grandmother I want Him for.

I wish her this Heaven: a bright red dress and a second chance to live, love and die.

I wish myself this replay: to be at the nursing home to catch you, to visit the hospice on the night you go.

Southerly

The cool change comes in just as you rest yourself down at the tram stop, no fight in you to walk. Bloody sun is seething behind clouds or smoke, its unholy halo fluorescent. A storm threatens, but after days of dry heat that downpour would be welcome. You notice a cyclist waiting patiently for the green light—gold hair wafting, blue cotton dress flapping, the curve of her shoulders still young. She reminds you of the girl you were, lifts you out of small-minded matters, takes you back to torpid evenings spent in another self—Istanbul foreign and dreamy, ice cream dripping from sticky crepes, hungry looks from Anatolian men, antique books at the night market, and all those lights beckoning across the Bosphorus. When the first drops burst, splashing your sandalled feet, drumming darkening concrete—you are no longer angry at the sun, your lover, or any of them.

Carriage

Grace and dignity
don't come easy.
You will try to be your best
and it is the trying
that matters.
You are your mother's dogged daughter
but do not react in haste.
Find Frankl's gap.
Stop. Look about. Grow
a bigger heart
like the enlarged muscle that pumped
hard in the chest of your dearest dead one.
Carry yourself somewhere worth going.
Do work that counts if you can.
The world is full of animals;
let the right ones in.

There will be missed-beat moments

when you'll see
the tea-towel drop
in slow
motion

ken
what life
doesn't have in store
for you
what the spiral
has spun
out

doors
you must pass
through
then close
legs
that aren't fast
enough

fish
you'll forget
till they float
to the top of the tank
the cruelty
of human
carelessness

the way things
end
then begin again
differently

Afterword

Although I have experienced sexual harassment and assault, I have always considered myself extremely fortunate for escaping greater harm, both physically and psychologically. However, the years have not made me feel easier about the many uncomfortable experiences I have endured as a woman. I have become increasingly exasperated, appalled and saddened by the plight of women in our world. This collection answers back to the popular myth that considers misogyny as perpetrated by the rare man or 'monster' who does not represent the wider state of modern masculinity. These poems illustrate how sexist attitudes and behaviours persistently infiltrate female experience, from childhood and throughout adulthood, in private and public, with family and friends as well as strangers, and that this sexism is perpetuated by ordinary men (and women) in mundane, tedious, everyday ways. Misogyny is ubiquitous and banal almost to the point of invisibility and the fact that so much of it is considered harmless is what makes it so dangerous. Even minor instances of discrimination affect women's mental health and financial wellbeing, profoundly and increasingly over time. Furthermore, patriarchal colonialist attitudes continue to enable abhorrent abuse of animals and wanton destruction of the environment. It is my hope that these poems might raise awareness of ecofeminist concerns and challenge readers to recognise themselves and their loved ones (human and non-human) in these pages and reconsider their attitudes, actions, and inactions in response to our contemporary crisis of climate and culture.

Acknowledgements

Firstly, I acknowledge the Peramangk and Kaurna peoples as the custodians of the unceded lands on which I live and work. I recognise and respect their cultural heritage, beliefs and relationship with the land and I pay my respects to their elders past, present and emerging. My sincere gratitude to Arts SA for funding the writing of this manuscript, and to Varuna the National Writers' House for providing a place to edit it in partnership with Writers SA. I want to express my huge appreciation to Shane Strange, Es Foong, and the team at Recent Work Press for believing in this manuscript and facilitating its transformation into a physical artefact. Thanks to Kate Larsen for creating a haunting trailer and writing a stellar review. I would like to recognise the CEO of Australian Poetry Jacinta Le Plastrier for her enduring service to this art form. Many thanks to Dr Rachael Mead for reading manuscript drafts and sharing insightful advice. I would like to acknowledge the poets who have taught and mentored me over the years, including Judith Beveridge, Chris Wallace-Crabbe, Deb Westbury, Jordie Albiston, Mark Tredinnick, Kevin Brophy, and Jan Owen. I would also like to remember my high school English teacher Josie Mitchell for the warmth of her encouragement. I am grateful to my family who have supported my love of literature since I was a child, and to my friends who have accompanied me on this writing journey for so many years. Thank you especially to those who have purchased this book and who continue to prioritise supporting and reading Australian poetry in an increasingly costly and busy world.

Several of these poems were published as earlier versions:

'Killer', *Borderless: A transnational anthology of feminist poetry*, Recent Work Press, 2021.
'The future we want is already gone', 'what if you made your own cage' and 'Sanctum', *Burrow* Issue 3, 2021.
'Phoning home', *Cordite Poetry Review*, 95: Earth, 2020.

'Prayer for the girl who is not a feminist' and 'Fucking Lucky', *Southerly,* Vol. 79.1, 2019.

'Working girl', *Mascara Literary Review,* Issue 24, 2019.

'The Emotional Astronomer', *Meanjin,* Summer 2017.

'Doppler Shift' and 'there will be missed-beat moments', *Meniscus* Vol. 5, Issue 2, 2017.

'Southerly', *Australian Poetry Journal,* Vol. 4, No 1. 2014.

'Hornet in my kitchen', *The Light Painters,* Katharine Susannah Prichard Writers' Centre, 2014.

'Running into your ex', *Best Australian Poems,* 2014 and *Australian Love Poems,* 2013.

Dr Bronwyn Lovell is a poet, novelist, and scholar of science fiction and space history. Her essays have been published by *Science Fiction Film and Television, The Journal of Feminist Scholarship,* and the National Gallery of Victoria. Her poetry has appeared in anthologies including *Best Australian Poems, Australian Love Poems,* and *Borderless: A transnational anthology of feminist poetry,* as well as journals including *Meanjin, Southerly, Antipodes,* and *Strange Horizons.* She has won the Arts Queensland Val Vallis Award and was runner-up for the inaugural RMIT/Giramondo Speculate Prize. Her work has been shortlisted for the Dorothy Hewett Award, Judith Wright Poetry Prize, Fair Australia Prize, Newcastle Poetry Prize, Bridport Prize, and Montreal International Poetry Prize. She holds an executive certificate in space studies from the International Space University has been commissioned to write poetry for the Australian Space Agency. She teaches creative writing and screen studies at the University of South Australia. Her verse novel, *Between Worlds,* is published by the University of Western Australia Publishing. *In Bed with Animals* is her first poetry collection.

www.ingramcontent.com/pod-product-compliance
Ingram Content Group Australia Pty Ltd
76 Discovery Rd, Dandenong South VIC 3175, AU
AUHW020639050325
407891AU00002B/12

9 780645 356342